VICTORIA JUSTICE

Amie Jane Leavitt

Mitchell Lane
PUBLISHERS

P.O. Box 196
Hockessin, Delaware 19707
Visit us on the web: www.mitchelllane.com
Comments? email us: mitchelllane@mitchelllane.com

Mitchell Lane

PUBLISHERS

Printing 1 2 3 4 5 6 7 8 9

A Robbie Reader
Contemporary Biography

Abigail Breslin	Albert Pujols	Alex Rodriguez
Aly and AJ	Amanda Bynes	AnnaSophia Robb
Ashley Tisdale	Brenda Song	Brittany Murphy
Charles Schulz	Dakota Fanning	Dale Earnhardt Jr.
David Archuleta	Demi Lovato	Donovan McNabb
Drake Bell & Josh Peck	Dr. Seuss	Dwayne "The Rock" Johnson
Dylan & Cole Sprouse	Eli Manning	Emily Osment
Emma Watson	Hilary Duff	Jaden Smith
Jamie Lynn Spears	Jennette McCurdy	Jesse McCartney
Jimmie Johnson	Johnny Gruelle	Jonas Brothers
Jordin Sparks	Justin Bieber	Keke Palmer Larry
Fitzgerald	LeBron James	Mia Hamm
Miley Cyrus	Miranda Cosgrove	Raven-Symoné
Selena Gomez	Shaquille O'Neal	Story of Harley-Davidson
Syd Hoff	Taylor Lautner	Tiki Barber
Tom Brady	Tony Hawk	Victoria Justice

Library of Congress Cataloging-in-Publication Data
Leavitt, Amie Jane.
  Victoria Justice / by Amie Jane Leavitt.
    p. cm. — (A robbie reader)
  Includes filmography.
  Includes bibliographical references and index.
  ISBN 978-1-58415-902-5 (library bound)
  1. Justice, Victoria, 1993– — Juvenile literature. 2. Actors—United States—Biography.
  3. Singers—United States—Biography. I. Title.
  PN2287.J87L43 2010
  791.4502'8092—dc22
  [B]
                                                                                    2010011156

ABOUT THE AUTHOR: Amie Jane Leavitt is an accomplished author and photographer. She graduated from Brigham Young University as an education major and has since taught all subjects and grade levels in both private and public schools. She is an adventurer who loves to travel the globe in search of interesting story ideas and beautiful places to capture on film. She has written dozens of books for kids, including *Taylor Lautner*, *Abigail Breslin*, and *Miley Cyrus* for Mitchell Lane Publishers. Amie enjoys writing about people who are achieving their dreams. For this reason, she particularly enjoyed researching and writing this book on Victoria Justice. For further information on this author, visit her official website: http://www.amiejaneleavitt.com.

PUBLISHER'S NOTE: The following story has been thoroughly researched and to the best of our knowledge represents a true story. While every possible effort has been made to ensure accuracy, the publisher will not assume liability for damages caused by inaccuracies in the data, and makes no warranty on the accuracy of the information contained herein. This story has not been authorized or endorsed by Victoria Justice.

TABLE OF CONTENTS

Words in **bold** type can be found in the glossary.

As a successful actress, Victoria Justice has made many friends in show business. She and Taylor Lautner met a long time ago. Despite rumors, they have never dated. "I've been busy working on my show and he's busy being a heartthrob," she said in a *J-14* interview.

Victorious

Victoria sat on the plane, waiting for it to land in Miami, Florida. She was on her way home from California to visit her grandmother. She had a lot on her mind that day. She looked out over the blue-green waters of the Atlantic and thought about her acting career. She had just started filming a new movie for Nickelodeon called *Spectacular!* She could not imagine being any happier than she felt right at that moment.

After the plane skidded to a stop on the runway, it made its way to the gate. Victoria gathered her things and strolled out into the terminal, checking her messages on her iPhone as she walked. She heard a message that made her suddenly stop. The big **executives** (ek-

ZEK-yoo-tivs) at Nickelodeon had seen her performance and had listened to her singing on *Spectacular!* They were very impressed with what they saw and heard. They were offering her the starring role on her very own television show!

Tammin Sursok, Simon Curtis, Victoria, and Nolan Funk all had parts in *Spectacular!* "Even though it was a Nickelodeon movie and I was a Nickelodeon girl . . . ," Victoria told *Girls' Life*, "I had to audition like everybody else. . . . It was not easy."

Victoria almost dropped her bags and screamed for joy. She said she just started "freaking out" right there in the airport. The people around her were probably a little confused by her reaction, but they must have known that something big had just happened for her.

Victoria did not completely understand how great this news really was until the first day of production. It just happened to be her **sweet sixteen** birthday.

"It was just so overwhelming to me," she told a reporter for *Girls' Life* in December 2009. "I couldn't believe that I was standing there with all of these people, and it was for my TV show. It was everything I had worked so hard for, for all this time, and it made me feel so good. I burst into tears because I was so incredibly happy."

Victoria began working at the age of eight. "It wasn't one of those things where my parents were like, go out there and model, we want you to work. It was always me at a young age wanting to [work]," Victoria told *J-14* in April 2010.

Born a Hollywood Star

Victoria Dawn Justice was one of the first babies to come into the world in Hollywood, Florida, on February 19, 1993. She was born just three minutes after midnight. Her parents were Zack and Serene Justice.

Some people are just born to perform. Victoria seems to be one of them. From a very young age, she loved being in front of people, singing and dancing. "I have always been the kid who at family gatherings would put on my **tutu** and my mom's lipstick, perform and make everybody watch me," she told *Girls' Life* in December 2009.

When Victoria was eight years old, she was watching television one afternoon. She saw a **commercial** (kuh-MER-shul) that really interested her—a commercial for potato chips. The kid showcasing the product was just about her age. Victoria called her mother into the room and said, "I want to be on TV." She thought it looked easy and fun.

Victoria's mother knew her daughter had a lot of talent. After all, she had watched hundreds of Victoria's performances. She made an appointment for her daughter with a modeling agency in Miami. The agency instantly saw **potential** (poh-TEN-shul) in Victoria and gave her a **contract** (KON-trakt).

Her first **audition** (aw-DIH-shun) was for a television commercial in 2001. She wouldn't be selling potato chips, though. Instead, the commercial was for a milk flavoring product made by Ovaltine. "I actually took an Ovaltine canister with me to the audition, and I guess they liked me because I wound up booking the job!"

It was all uphill from there. Over the next couple of years, she appeared in 30 television

Victoria likes to spend time with her little sister, Madison Reed. "She's at that age where I've experienced all of these things that she's going through, so I can help her with a lot, especially the boys," she told *Girls' Life* in 2009.

commercials and magazine advertisements for such big-name companies as the Gap, Guess, and Ralph Lauren. She wondered, Will I ever act in anything else?

Victoria has always been willing to try new things. In 2006, she had the chance to hold an anaconda (an-uh-KON-duh), one of the largest snakes in the world.

From Hollywood to Hollywood

Victoria definitely was not shy in front of cameras. At one job, the photographers wanted one of the girls to kiss one of the boys. This was the limit for most of the girls on the set, but not for Victoria! She recalled the event to a reporter for *Girls' Life*: "All the girls were like, 'I don't want to do it. Cooties!' And I was like, 'I'll do it! I'll do it!' I've always been pretty outgoing."

This willingness to try new things was the perfect attitude for climbing the ladder of success in Hollywood. Yet if Victoria really wanted to reach her full potential, she would have to trade her beloved hometown of

Victoria is close with her mother, who is almost always with her on set. "I ask my mom for advice on everything, from my hair to work-related stuff to what I should say to a boy. . . . My mom is the one person I trust," she told *Family Circle* in 2010.

Hollywood, Florida, for the bigger and busier Hollywood, California.

In the summer of 2003, she boarded a plane with her family and flew to the West Coast. Within just three weeks, she landed her first television role on the popular WB series *Gilmore Girls*. She would play the part of Jill on the Halloween episode titled "The Hobbit, the Sofa, and Digger Stiles."

Victoria told *The Hollywood Reporter* in 2005, "I had one line. I was dressed in a heavy robe, and it was 103 degrees, but I didn't care. I was so thrilled to be on the set." That was a defining moment in Victoria's life. She knew she was born to be a star.

Over the next few months, she landed small parts in several **independent** (in-dih-PEN-dent) **films**. The first was called *Fallacy* (FAL-uh-see) with Gary Busey. The second was *When Do We Eat?* with Michael Lerner, Leslie Ann Warren, and Jack Klugman.

In the fall, Victoria's family went back to Florida. Victoria continued modeling and

Since Victoria moved to California, she has made friends with other teen stars, such as Miranda Cosgrove from *iCarly* and Keke Palmer from *True Jackson, VP.* "My favorite things about California are the mountains, Malibu, and the waves at the beach," she told *Scholastic News* in 2006.

landed some important contracts, but the cameras of California kept calling her name.

The next summer, the family packed their bags and journeyed west for a second time. Once again, it was only a matter of weeks before Victoria found work. She was featured on an AOL commercial and in two more independent films. The first was *My Purple Fur Coat* and the second was *Mary,* for which she had the lead role of Stella. This film became a hit at the Sundance Film Festival in January 2005.

While she and her family were in California, they decided that Victoria should audition for a **prestigious** (pres-TIH-jus) performing arts school. She did very well in her audition and was accepted into the school's musical theater program. With jobs and school all lined up, Victoria's family finally decided that Hollywood, California, was where they should stay.

Dan Schneider (left) has written and produced several popular shows for Nickelodeon. He created *Drake and Josh*, *iCarly*, *Zoey 101*, and *Victorious*. "Dan gets teenagers and gets what's cool and doesn't talk down to kids," Victoria told *USA Today* in 2010. "I'm very grateful to [him.]"

Zoey 101

In September 2004, Victoria landed a guest spot in the new Disney Channel series *The Suite Life of Zack and Cody*, which would air the following March. She had so much fun, she wrote on her web site, that "for a long time afterwards I would visit the set almost every week, when they would have their live studio audience performances on Tuesdays."

The following year, Victoria found roles in both television and film. She appeared as Thalia Thompson on the WB series *Everwood*, and then as Holly in the movie *The Garden*. In May 2005, she played Rose on the Hallmark Christmas television movie *Silver Bells*. She wrote on her web site: "I was rehearsing the song for the choir scene [in *Silver Bells*] when I received the phone call that I had booked the role of Lola on *Zoey 101*. So when you see that big smile on my face in the choir scene . . . you'll know why."

The role of Lola Martinez was Victoria's biggest gig yet. "I loved playing Lola because she was so glamorous," Victoria later told *Supermodels Unlimited.* "I was only twelve at the time when I landed the role of Lola, so for me it was a dream come true. I loved her clothes and her sense of style. . . . She always looked great and had no problem speaking her mind. . . . I will always feel honored to have been cast to play her."

Victoria and the other kids on the show became really good friends. "We would go out to eat when we were done or just hang out in someone's car and talk for hours. It was usually Erin [Sanders], Matt [Underwood], and [me] in a booth at Marie Callender's Restaurant talking for three hours! We had so much fun."

Zoey 101 aired for three years on Nickelodeon. Victoria was really sad to see it end. "I had spent three seasons on that series, and we had all grown up a lot, and gone through so many things together. I have amazing memories that I will always treasure," she told *Supermodels Unlimited*.

Yet life for Victoria wasn't over after *Zoey 101*. She landed the part of Tammi on Nick's *Spectacular!*, a made-for-television movie that aired in 2009. This opportunity gave her a chance to sing. Next to acting, music is one of Victoria's passions. The bigwigs at Nickelodeon were impressed. They decided to showcase this young star in her own series, called *Victorious*. Victoria would star with Ariana Grande, Daniella Monet, Matt Bennett, Elizabeth Gillies, and Leon Thomas, and the show would air in March 2010.

When they were on *Zoey 101*, Victoria and Erin Sanders helped raise money for APe Action. Animals, People and Environment Action (APe Action) helps make people aware of how they can make the world a better place for people and animals.

Fun Times

Victoria may be a famous television and movie star, but she's also a typical kid in many ways. "In my spare time I hang out with my sister [Maddie], my friends, and my family. I like to swim, ice-skate; I love to read and I sing **karaoke** [kayr-ee-OH-kee]. I like anything that keeps me active and that involves my friends and family," she told *Starry Constellation Magazine* in 2006.

Victoria's favorite foods are Cuban, Greek, and Italian, but her favorite meal is either **filet mignon** (fih-LAY min-YON) or prime rib with cream of spinach and a loaded baked potato. She loves decaf caramel **cappuccinos** (kah-puh-CHEE-nohs), strawberry milk shakes with extra whipped cream, Ben & Jerry's Cherry Garcia and Breyers Rocky Road ice creams. Her favorite beach is in Hollywood, Florida. "It has a three-and-a-half-mile boardwalk, where you can bike, Rollerblade, scooter, skateboard, or whatever you're into," she said. "The water's not cold, and it's really blue-green. It's so cool!"

Victoria is a huge music fan and also loves **vintage** (VIN-tidj) movies. The walls of

Victoria loves hanging out with friends and goofing around. She loves playing Guitar Hero III: Legends of Rock, but her favorite hobbies are walking her dogs and riding her bike.

her bedroom are covered with posters of the Beatles, Marilyn Monroe, and Audrey Hepburn. She also takes her iPod with her everywhere. As well as being a successful actress, Victoria is also a really good student. She is a **perfectionist** (per-FEK-shuh-nist) and tries her best to get straight As in her classes.

Ever since Victoria broke into the entertainment business, she has tried to spend some of her time helping others. While she was on *Zoey 101*, she and her castmates went to many charity events. She has also helped on her own, too. She has done work for the Make-A-Wish Foundation, Variety's Power of Youth, and DoSomething.org.

Victoria has a lot of goals, such as winning an Oscar—the highest award in the film industry. She would also like to be successful enough that she can be "choosy" about the roles she accepts. She told *Supermodels Unlimited*, "I would like to have a career that I can be really proud of. I love doing both drama and comedy, but my preference is probably comedy right now. I love having fun and I love to laugh."

In April 2006, a reporter for *American Girl* magazine asked her if she had any advice for other kids who want to get into the acting business. She said, "Enroll in some classes or join your local theater group. Once you find

J-14 reported: Before Victoria met Justin Bieber, a fan asked her if she would kiss him. She replied, "First of all, I don't know him, so it would be really random if I ran up and kissed him. I think I would freak him out and security would definitely be all over me."

Victoria loves performing. She hopes to eventually have a solo album with some of her own music on it. "I'm so excited to write my own music and to…have kids be able to relate to my music."

an acting class you like, stay with it. It's a great experience getting up in front of a large group of people. It helps you gain confidence."

Whether you decide to try acting or some other career, you should definitely take an example from a page of Victoria's life. Get out there and try, never give up, and you'll be able to accomplish more than you ever dreamed was possible.

CHRONOLOGY

1993 Victoria Dawn Justice is born in Hollywood, Florida, on February 19.

1996 Her sister, Madison (Maddie), is born.

2001 Victoria decides she wants to be an actor. Her mother enrolls her at a modeling agency in Miami. She acts in an Ovaltine commercial.

2003 Victoria and her family decide to move to Hollywood, California, so that Victoria can pursue her acting career. She gets her first real Hollywood gig when she lands the role as Jill in *Gilmore Girls*.

2005 She lands her big role as Lola Martinez in the Nickelodeon series *Zoey 101*. The series continues until 2008. She plays Young Nikki in *When Do We Eat?*, Rebecca in *The Suite Life of Zack and Cody*, Rose in *Silver Bells*, and Stella in *Mary*.

2006 She plays Thalia Thompson in *Everwood*, and Holly in *The Garden*.

2007 She releases a single titled "A Thousand Miles."

2009 She plays Betsy in *The Kings of Appletown*; Vivian in *True Jackson, VP*; Shelby Marx in *iCarly*; and Tammi in *Spectacular!* She is featured on the sound track for *Spectacular!*

2010 She plays Jordan Sands in the television production *The Boy Who Cried Werewolf* and Eris Fairy in *The Troop*. *Victorious* debuts on March 27.

FILMOGRAPHY

2010	*Victorious* (TV)
	The Boy Who Cried Werewolf (TV movie)
	The Troop (TV)
2009	*The Kings of Appletown* (TV)
	True Jackson, VP (TV)
	iCarly (TV)
	Spectacular! (TV movie)
2006	*Everwood* (TV)
	The Garden
2005–2008	*Zoey 101* (TV)
2005	*When Do We Eat?*
	The Suite Life of Zack and Cody (TV)
	Mary
	Silver Bells (TV movie)
2004	*Fallacy*
2003	*Gilmore Girls* (TV)

DISCOGRAPHY

| 2009 | *Spectacular!* —Sound track (featured) |
| 2007 | "A Thousand Miles" (Single) |

FIND OUT MORE

Books and Magazine Articles
Bloom, Ronny. *Victoria Justice* (Get the Scoop). New York: Price Stern Sloan, 2009.
"Victoria 101." *American Girl*, April 2006.
"Victoria Justice." *Gossip Teen*. n.d.
      http://gossipteen.com/category/victoria-justice/
"Victoria Justice." *Scholastic News*, Star Spotlight: n.d.
      http://teacher.scholastic.com/scholasticnews/mtm/
      starspotlight.asp?sf=justice
"Victoria Justice." *Teen Magazine*, Spring 2006.
"Victoria Justice." *Tiger Beat*, March 2006.
"Victoria Justice Interview." n.d.
      http://www.kidzworld.com/article/7291-victoria-justice-interview

FIND OUT MORE

Works Consulted

Forr, Amanda, Patricia McNamara, and Vicki Arkoff. "GL What's Hot." *Girls' Life*,
February/March 2009, Vol. 15, Issue 4, pp. 40–42.

Keveney, Bill. "Nickelodeon Builds Dynamic Duo." *USA Today*. http://www. usatoday.
com/life/television/news/2010-06-04-nick04_ST_N.htm

Martinez, Patty A. "Talent Show: Teen Celebrities and Their Dedicated Moms." *Family
Circle*, May 2010. http://www. familycircle.com/teen/parenting/
teen-celebrities-and-their-moms/?page=1

Morreale, Marie. *Star Spotlight*. http://teacher.scholastic.com/scholasticnews/mtm/
starspotlight.asp?sf=justice

Scarola, Danielle. "Victoria Secrets." *Girls' Life*, December 2009/January 2010,
Vol. 16, Issue 3, pp. 46–49.

Shafii, Renee. "Victoria 101." *Supermodels Unlimited*, Hollywood Edition, 2008.

Sheehan, Brian. "Victoria Justice: Nick's New Face." *Daily Variety*, October 3, 2005, p.
A60.

"Showbiz Kids." *The Hollywood Reporter Special Edition*, November 18, 2005.

Steinburg, Jamie. "Victoria Justice." *Starry Constellation Magazine*.
http://www.starrymag.com/content.asp?ID=1075&CATEGORY=Interviews

"To Tell the Tooth." *Girls' Life*, February 2006, Vol. 12, Issue 4, p. 88.

" 'Zoey 101's' Victoria Justice Gets Own Series." *Access Hollywood*, August 13, 2008.
http://www.accesshollywood.com/zoey-101s-victoria-justice-gets-own-series_
article_10828

Videos

J-14 Interview. http:// modoration.com/2010/04/27/
victoria-justice-i-did-not-date-taylor-lautner/

"Victoria Justice Interview with GratedCheese.com," 2007.
http://video.google.com/videoplay?docid=-4838691690390511934&ei=KyF6S
5vQAZSYqQOX5YWjBw&q=victoria+justice&hl=en#

"Victorious." http://www.youtube.com/watch?v=7dmrFeb0kZc

"Victoria Justice Interview." *Teen.com*, April 10, 2009.
http://www.youtube.com/watch?v=GL0hFmuJhDo

"Victoria Justice Gives Teen Fans Advice!" June 1, 2009.
http://www.youtube.com/watch?v=yb69pV3uvns&feature=related

"Victoria's Best Advice." July 22, 2009.
http://www.youtube.com/watch?v=5P5cvYwVUpE&feature=related

"Victoria Justice and Simon Curtis at Merry Christmas, Drake & Josh!" December 2,
2008. http://www.youtube.com/watch?v=_x_tZ7UBASw

On the Internet

Official Website
http://www.victoriajustice.net

Victoria's Official YouTube Channel
http://www.youtube.com/victoriajustice4all#p/a/u/2/TmskegO-Jy0

Victorious on Nick
http://www.nick.com/shows/victorious/

Victoria on Twitter: @VictoriaJustice

GLOSSARY

audition (aw-DIH-shun)—A tryout for a part in a play or movie.

cappuccino (kah-puh-CHEE-noh)—Strong coffee served with steamed cream.

commercial (kuh-MER-shul)—An advertisement on television.

contract (KON-trakt)—A document between two or more people that details an agreement between them.

executive (ek-ZEK-yoo-tiv)—One of the top managers in a company.

filet mignon (fih-LAY min-YON)—The center cut of steak that is very tender and expensive.

independent (in-dih-PEN-dent) **film**— A movie made by people who do not work for a large film company.

karaoke (kayr-ee-OH-kee)—Singing into a microphone to recorded music.

perfectionist (per-FEK-shuh-nist)—Someone who does not allow for mistakes.

potential (poh-TEN-shul)—A measure of what is possible.

prestigious (pres-TIH-jus)—Held in high regard.

sweet sixteen—A party for a girl who is turning sixteen years old.

tutu (TOO-too)—A type of skirt used by dancers that is made out of mesh material.

vintage (VIN-tidj)—Something from a distant time period.

INDEX